All Over the Place

Robertson Greene

No part of this publication may be reproduced, stored in a retrieval system, or transmitted, in any form
or by any means, electronic, mechanical, photocopying, recording, or otherwise, without the written
permission of the author.

First published by Dog Ear Publishing
4011 Vincennes Road
Indianapolis, IN 46268
www.dogearpublishing.net

ISBN: 1-4575-6427-0

This book is printed on acid-free paper.
Printed in the United States of America

For my Mother; my best friend and greatest inspiration.

- Love Nunn

&

For my lovers; my best friends' and beautiful disasters

- Love Rob

1971

I met her
Orleans Parish
Josephine Street
1971 while walking
Up the street headed
To the corner store
For a cold drink
Preparing to catch the bus
Cross the river to Algiers
Her name was Pearl Anne
Last name Glapion
I was taken aback by her hourglass
Shape and her dark skin
Which she cleaned gently
With Noxzema before bed
She became my everything
In that moment and thereafter
We were free to be us
Lovers of love
Gentle on our minds
Pearl Anne cooked and turned
The darkest moments to sunshine
We rode the trolleys up and down
Canal Street while cooling off
With cold cups we got for a nickel
Over at the sweet shop ran
By Miss Erma on Ursuline who usually
Sold the hot suppers on Friday's
We loved each other
Every day was us together

Being one shadow
Living in one time
Moments were endless
Even as I stood over
Her grave as she no longer
Could fight the battles of illness
That lined her breast
I loved her still
My everything
Like the moment we first met
Orleans Parish
Josephine Street
1971

A Man In Danger

I have loved a lot of faces
And the love is all the same
I have raced in many races
But I never won a game
Never had a taste for honey
But vinegar is my thing
More in love with the money
Some say that it's a shame
I'm a man in danger
But danger is funny
Living the way that I do
Just a man in danger
Danger of loving
I live with so much attitude
In silence I want to holler
I've been called a devilish man
Try to buy me with your dollar
Yet I'm back in escrow again
It's just a valor of honor
I'm just a lover of pain
In hell I have a condo
Lucifer knows my name
I'm a man in danger
But danger is funny
Living the way that I do
Just a man in danger
Danger of loving
I live with so much attitude
A man in danger

Just call me quite cunning
Happy with just being blue
I'm a man in danger
But danger is funny
Living the way that I do
Just a man in danger
Danger of loving
I live with so much attitude

A Slave Story

Just like those lashings
My brother Solomon
Took for no reason at all
I am beat beyond
How much longer before I can dance on the
Heels of the north star
Solomon promised me that one day a better life
Would be for us both but he never made it
Took his own life one day
Out back behind the shed
Took Big Man's riffle and let off one shot to his temple
Momma was numb and
I was scared to wonder if I was next because the lashings
Were worse than forever burning in hell
Lord knows I'm beat
Feeling old and withered
Wondering If there is a God
How could he let this be
How could he love them and not us
Momma and Solomon was all I had
Come one Sunday Momma didn't wake up
Lola said she died in her sleep
That's how come she knew Momma was an angel
She had the biggest smile on her face as she laid peacefully
I'm sure she was with Solomon now
Running peacefully and carrying a smile
As long as the Mississippi
Now the lashings are coming more frequent
Almost every time the sun rises
My skin just falls off my back

I'm pained
Can barely open my mind to believe
That there is a better life
Maybe the north start ain't nothing but
A fairytale passed on down to my kind
Maybe Big Man and all his people planted
That seed in the ears of everyone that
Worked the fields just so that they can catch
One of us trying to chase an illusion one night
Momma and Solomon are gone
Lord I tell you
I may as well be gone too

A Slave's Dream

I'm gonna run on away from here
Goodbye
I'm gonna live on with no fear
So long
I'm gonna follow the North Star
Until I can get along so far
Until strange fruit are no longer no more
I'm gonna run on away from here
Goodbye
I'm gonna live on with no fear
So long
I'm gonna follow the North Star
Until Heaven has become my home
Forever sang a freedom song
I'm gonna run on away from here
Goodbye
I'm gonna live on with no fear
So long
I'm gonna follow the North Star
Until I floats a river far
Though my back has many scars
I'm gonna run on away from here
Goodbye

Ain't No Way

Ain't no way
God knows
On everything
That measures
Up to love
Ain't no way
Could I ever
Consider
Reconsider
That is
Allowing for my
Soul to lie down
Next to a void again
I rather be . . . .
Than to be . . . .
Just
Ain't no way

Alexis Paige

Alexis Paige
Woman of modern taste
Slender in frame
Silhouette of Vanity Fair
Yet she still is trapped in
Times where time hasn't
Been clear on a summers day
The envy of the courtyards
The black man's trophy but
She wasn't a cookie cutter
Not in her interest to be
What she saw her mother
Her mother's mother become
Alexis Paige
Knows no boundaries
Relentless like a river's wild
More hustle than any dice game
Going on in the alleyways of
A fish fry on a Friday night
Yet she is lady in presence
Alone because she wants to
Bold because she has to
Though I don't see much of her
I reckon I'll always love her
I can only imagine she's doing
What she does best
Being the lady she knows how to be
Unconventional

Avant Garde
Strolling the runways of the avenues
Smelling of vanilla and cinnamon but
Crisp like a gardenia
Nevertheless
Alexis Paige
Is who she is
I reckon I'll always love her

All Over the Place

I'm all over
All over the place
In between highs and lows
Drunken off of time
Loved
In love
Not so loved
Appearing to be awkward
In a life where I am endangered
Sinning from coast to coast
Not even thinking about much
I want to be a rocket to blast off into the galaxy
Be a star amongst them all
Much rather lie in the grass
And stare at the floating clouds
With their animal shapes
I'm all over
All over the place
Stopped making sense of that
Many seasons ago
I wonder why blue is my favorite color
Mangoes make me smile like a child all over again
Mary Jane is my lover
Comforts me when I need a pillow
It's just like I don't know
I'm complete
Intertwined with complexity
Though I'm satisfied
With a bowl of corn grits
Topped off with butter and cheese

I want to be in Africa
Lust in Rome
Make great strides in Chile
Play music in Memphis
Then bring it back home
So I can dream while
Listening to Nina
Crooning to Otis
Getting down to the
Sounds of Celia
All the way to wondering
Why Langston didn't let his
Dream defer or why Ray
Gained sight through the
Art of song
I'm all over
All over the place

Ambrosia

Say you want to be with me
Come home to it
Let's do it
Treat me like a piece of meat
Feed you evenings and mornings
If what I feel is a crime
Guess I'm bout to do a lifetime
For giving you everything
Your lips are sweet as ambrosia
Waiting for you to come over
Sweet as ambrosia
I just want to be for you
Sweet as ambrosia
I just want to be....
I just want to be....
I just want to be....
For you
I won't tell no lie....
I won't tell no lie....
I won't tell no lie....
I won't tell no lie....
As I always told you
Your lips are sweet as ambrosia
Waiting for you to come over
Say you want to be with me
Come home to it
Let's do it

America, You Bitch

Living in a time
Where people often
Die by the hands of
Supremacist minds
A being of color is
Nothing but a hate crime
Recent executive order wants
The Brown man to
Stay behind the lines
Claiming that women
Are only worth what's between
Their legs as a treasured prize
Anglo fools running this country
No nothing of struggle because
Off of the strength of colored people
They were afforded a privileged life
Feels like all mankind could die
At any moment an attack
Can come by plane again
From the enemy's pride
Being a part of the fifty
Has been a Jim Crow ride
Modern day strange fruit
Hangs on the mantle of
A grand wizard's tribe
Only to prove that we
Are still divided by a fault
Carrying picket signs

Undone the last sixty years
In the blink of an eye
Yet they say we should
Be grateful to be here and
Eat a slice of the
American Pie

An Addict to a Pipe

I'm emotional for you
Last night was everything
Time is what we gave one another
You told me things
I confessed to you
Now today my thoughts are seasoned
With the aftershocks from our makings
Repeatedly under the silver moon
I just want more
I hope that's not wanting too much
In fear that I am hooked
Like an addict to a pipe

Anxiety

The walls are caving in
I can't even breathe
Feel like I can lie down
And die
Help me someone please
Crazy thoughts in my head
My eyes are fire red
My skin is crawling
Fetal position
Like in my mother's womb
Staring at the walls
I'm starting to hate this room
Silent prayers to myself
I'm afraid to even dream
Pills are not working
My sins
Are my friends
I can't do this
I just can't breathe

Assiduously

I've been doing it
For a long time now
Without any regrets
Without any reservations,
None what so ever
It was easy for me to do so
As easy as a summer breeze
I loved you assiduously
With no convincing
Would have stood before anyone
If I was forced to
But today all I have is
Broken mirrors
Needs that are in need
And a strong memory
Of what your fragrance smelled
Like over me
But as it still stands
I loved you assiduously

Au revoir Desdemona

Love I don't want to hear about
How getting up every day to provide
A life for us has caused you
To reside in the arms of another
Finding solace in the realm of a being
That doesn't resemble me by far
Or how I left you no choice because
I was so selfish to work what felt like
A million hours
For us to have
For you to be without worry
For us to be secure
For you to wake up each day with a creaseless face
I don't want to hear about
How I left you no choice
So now that I've made it to the crossroads
In this thing we call us
I've decided to venture off
To do all the things that makes me whole
The things I've forgotten
The things that were lost
The identity that vanished when you came
Well you have left me no choice
Though it's a transition that will
Take some getting use to
You have left me no choice
But to spread my wings and live
Live how I want to
Live just for me

Free of duties
Released from discontentment
Without any thoughts of
What I should be doing for you
There is no hate in my being
When I think of you
I just prefer not to think of you
This day moving on
Au revoir Desdemona

Aunt Delores

Aunt Delores sat on the front porch of her Magazine Street home
Hair always in rollers and a can of beer in which she always
Sipped out of a straw painting her fingernails as the record player
belted out the sounds of Aretha Franklin's *Ain't No Way* and
Aunt Delores sung along in tune
Brought back memories of yesteryear when she and Uncle James
First married and he was a seaman and he loved
Aunt Delores the minute he laid eyes on her at Pontchatrain Beach
Months later they were married he would send home money and fancy
Gifts he picked up in his travels while Aunt Delores kept the house clean
Her beehive maintained and nails manicured that was always painted red
Uncle James was gone almost a year when Aunt Delores met Johnnie
    Armstrong
Tall and dark with a head full of conk one Saturday evening as she shopped
For a blouse at Krauss department store down on Canal Street and it was
    instant attraction
What man could have not looked at Delores Donsereaux as she passed and
    sashayed the way she did
I mean she was well kept and Uncle James made
Sure of that and everyone knew but temptation crept in and after days and
    nights
Of talking with Johnnie Armstrong Aunt Delores decided to let him come on
    over
One Friday night after she thought the neighbor's eyes were tending to their
    own business and
There was Johnnie Armstrong at the front door smelling of Stetson with that
    deep voice
That made Aunt Delores feel some kind of way and candles were lit and
    music was playing

One kiss led to another and another and before you knew it Aunt Delores
and Johnnie Armstrong

Were in bed making love through the night hours as she straddled him while
he filled her up with

His love potions as Uncle James picture stood there on the night stand and
Aunt Delores paid that

Picture of her husband that was away making a living for his wife no never
mind and just like that Morning came and birds chirped while the
lingering of stale loving was in the air

Beautiful Saturday morning as the sun crept in through the plantation
shutters while life

Outdoors began to move about and out of the blue arrived Uncle James with
roses in hand

A box with a gift and a face of smiles ready to see his woman after months
of separation and there goes Uncle James quietly walking up the stairs
excited to see Aunt Delores in her satin night gown

He purchased for her all the way from Chile and there he was standing in the
door while

Johnnie Armstrong and Aunt Delores lay there nakedly in the depths of sleep

Uncle James said nothing and he walked down the stairs almost quietly

Drop the roses at the front door and picked up his bags and walked out of
the house

Out of the roth iron gates and took one last look at the house on Magazine
Street that he paid for

And walked away to never return and that was thirty five years ago and ever
since he left Aunt Delores has been waiting for Uncle James to return
but he never does as she waits in vain

Listening to *Ain't No Way* because that was her and Uncle James favorite song

Awkward & Unanswered

I ask the questions
To what I want to know
Not in the light of prying
More so trying to secure
My spot in whatever I'm
Trying to be placed into
It all just comes across so
Vague with haze with no
Defined reason for
It's existence and I so
Despised being left in
The unknown and I take
Chances opening up my being
To the strangest of strangers
In hopes that my questions
Are answered clearly
However I come up short
The answers are still vague
Yet I'm still left to float
Away down whatever river
Feeling awkward and
Unanswered or am I
Taking on the awkwardness
Or the unanswered answers
Of someone else but it all
Just seems so undefined

Ball & Chain

Summer man
Church suit and all
Humming tunes
Of made up songs
Wish it would rain
He still won't complain
But that heat follows
Like a ball and chain
He has no time for dreaming
Beads of sweat has his skin gleaming
Summer man
Where the day catches you
Hard to smile
Complexion black-blue
Not sure where he going
He got something to do
All while the sun is a blaze
I wonder who he is
While followed by
The ball and chain
It's all a mental game
Crying shame
As hot as it is
Call a cab again
Or call a friend
Wish it would rain
Summer man
Heat follows
Like a ball and chain

Strange enough
The man never complains
Never winced
Nor cried aloud
Of what he can't
Skin color of motor oil
Dressed as if he's going
To a Baptist church wake
He humming tunes again
Walking at a fast pace
God knows where's the rain
Life may be after him
Like a ball and chain

Barcelona

I've never wanted it all
Just a bit and then some
Enough to where I could
Taste every bit in every bite
And today I've found that
I wanted red wine and olives
And somehow I was given
Barcelona, the home of
Gaudi's magnum opus and
My blood was immersed in
Sangria and I finally knew
Just what home felt like
I suddenly realized that the
Land of the free and the home
Of the brave was my yesterday
So therefore the affair was over
Barcelona is now my love
In motion and my song and
Dance and bare like the shores
Of Mar Bella and I couldn't deny
Its kisses and I want to make this
Easier for both parties
My back is towards you
Because I love you
No sense in anchoring you to my blues
Or even myself so I relinquish us
I love Barcelona
And right now I'm just not
Willing to give that

Up
Not for you
Not my love for you
Not for the land of the free
Not for the home of the brave

Being Just Fine

As age approaches I decided to Lay my worry down
And make plans that would keep
Us adjoined even in times of drear
Though this intertwined emotion
We're in is never easy
I couldn't think of any other place
I would rather be
Though you're not my everything
I don't believe we should be
You're just enough for me
Crazy as it may be
You have my blessings to stray off
Sometime an emotion as such
Calls for just that
Tomorrow is uncertain
So is next week for that matter
But as I stand before you and time
Professing only what God has given me
The courage to say
I feel nothing less than
Being just fine

Bipolar in Love

Cautiously love you
You're in love with me
We talk on Thursday's
We're mad on Monday's
You think I'm special
I give you much to think about
You hold back
You run me off
I'm never gone far
You want me
I can't stand you
In love with you
What is this all about
Confusing
At times abusing
Misleading
We're dangerous
In heat you give me lots
Of emotions
I got that potion
You got the notion
To give me all you got
We're drowning
It's worrying
We're special
We're good to go
Maybe it's a no go
We give us things that are
Rogue with doubt

You don't love me
I don't love you
Maybe it's crazy
I don't want no one but you
You say you love me
Do you love me
I love you
It's the truth
Sometimes our love
Is full of sugar and rot

Black Man

My nose is too big
My skin is too dark
My lips are too full
My hair is too kinky
Aren't I good enough
Are my hands and feet
Too rough
My waist size is wide
My stomach isn't flat
Society says I'm not
European enough
I'm too ethnic they say
As a matter of fact
I don't get offered
A song nor a dance
I believe Nina told
A story of her Aunt Sarah
Inflicted again and again
Much rather see me
Dressed in a constant pain
Can't even blame the man
For the ignorance of
The Brotha man
That won't even hold
The Sista's hand but
I'm too lanky in posture
Get paid cents by the hour
My chest isn't chiseled
I'm ashy like flour

Burnt biscuit
Jiggerboo
Tell me I need to
Take a bleach shower
However I'm not ashamed
I'm not in in pain
Not a manmade man
Each morning I rise
Only to face it all again
Black man
Inflicted again and again
Black man
I live him again and again
Black man
I don't consider it a loss
I don't know if it's a win

Black So and So

I don't give a damn
About your loving
Just as you didn't give
A damn about mines
And I won't hear your
Words that you're talking
They'll only turn out
To be another lie
So what's all these promises
That you're throwing
I never heard such
Garbage in my life
The sight of your face
Is so disgusting
You try to touch me
And I tell you never mind
You're a black....
You're a black....
A black so and so
And I want to really hurt
Your world right now
Old black....
Old fat....
I don't think we can
Work out
You just crazy
I don't give a damn
About your loving
Just as you didn't give
A damn about mines

Block Party

It was Saturday
We were at the block party
The smell of the meats
Bathing on the grill was in the air
The ole timers were laughing
While holding their pints in hand
The electric slide moved over the
Black bodies as the sun beamed down
On the abandoned tenement in the distance
The times were groovy
Painted with big afro's that were sheened
Platform shoes and Chuck Taylor's
Diana was wearing hot pants
Milton was over there shooting dice
An oasis in the hood
Far and few in between
Just like that there in the distance
Flashing lights doing the hustle
Then the music stopped
The dancing became frozen
Ora Lee comes from around the back
Of the old abandoned tenement
Screaming with clothes stained with
Red blood running and with one slipper on
Not realizing she lost the other
They killed Peanut that's all she kept saying
Merna ran towards Ora Lee because Peanut
Was her son and he had been carrying on
With Ora Lee for quite some time now

They were adjoined at the hips
Merna as well as everyone else knew
Something was wrong
Peanut was dead
The lights were still doing the hustle
The block party was over
Ended in Peanut's blood

Blow the Horn

Out of the night skies appears my dangling life trying to find a safe place to land and I just don't know where am I am, who am I for that matter; at this point. My many rhythms and the ways I can deliver a song sometimes sadden me because the blues overshadows the good things that I really have going on. I don't want to remember. Remembering is just holding box after box of all of the unwanted garbage filled things in one's life and I just don't want to remember. I use to be a big pot of gumbo, many flavors and you could never just pin-point how much of Cajun spices was in me; so everybody wanted a taste and like a damn fool I gave all of me. So now I am just as blain as a bowl of oatmeal without the brown sugars and raisins. I have no flavor. They took it all. And I survive off of wishing and hoping that the tune off of the saxophone is going to play a black man's song of hope and redemption. I can see it now as soon as the horn begins to play; my feet begin to tapping and stomping in a sign of relief and character. And all of black men would come out of their shells and broken wombs and join in on the party. Join in on the wave but the horn hasn't blown yet. The only horn I hear is the horns of the old beat up mustang that comes around every Saturday night to pick up the tender-roni across the street, and after she comes out; all dressed up and smelling of magnolia leaves and apple-butter, he pulls off into the alley way right down the block. Giving her the best date she could have ever imagined. Every time he would enter her she imagined four stars, as in four star restaurants, hotels and lives, like the white women on all of her favorite, unrealistic television shows. This can't be living for no one. All of us are sitting around waiting for the horn to blow. The golden horn; the saxophone. Don't you know I watched a lady sing on stage at a local joint and she was as pretty as Lena Horne herself but every time she sang, she didn't sing about shit. And I watched a Brotha stand on stage playing the dozens with the audience and I didn't crack a smile not once. I just wanted to hear some good ole music. The kind of music I could take home with me and hold in my perception for when times grew into drear. I wanted to dance and fly across the room in my zoot and pretend I was Cab himself. But the only thing I found was a few pennies in my pocket, and old love letter from Irene and a bus pass. Now where and the hell could I go with a few cents and picture of a bitch who left me. Robbed me. Yeah, she took all of my things. My mental and emotional stability. She took it all from me and all I have left is hopes and dreams and the night life, my life. Lord knows that's not much at all. Yea she took all of my shit. But she can have it though, I've gotten tired of being the bridge that helped get her across. I didn't make a police report nor did I go looking for her. I just blew away like a leaf in the crisp skies. So now I stand in the window in the front of this pawn shop and there I see a golden horn, a saxophone. I go in and lay out my few cents and tell the store clerk that these few pennies of mines is all that I have and beg to let me play. If I don't play, I won't live. I won't wake up from this dream and all I'll do is keep dangling and dangling like the head of a fetus swimming out of his mother's womb. Somebody please let me play. Pay for me, I'll pay you back. I have long legs, black as the pit from pole to pole type skin and a stern bite. If you think you can use any of these treasures, you can have it. I just want the saxophone so I can blow a tune and find my ways back on home.

Bobby as Fallon Called Him

Fallon was Geraldine's daughther
Her father Botchie paints houses up on the boulevard for Mister Seager
He was the white man that had a thing for black women and smothered pig
    feet
Fallon's skin was the color of nutmeg always smelling of Jean Nate'
Her beehive was always in place sort of a brown and burgundy
Fallon would take the number three bus all the way to the other side of town
So that no one would see her enjoying the company of Mister Seager
She called him Bobby
Her father Botchie would go ape ballistic if he knew his only daughter was
    enjoying
The company of a white man in the heart of racial tensions and especially if
    it's Mister Seager
Somehow Fallon didn't pay her father no never mind
She was just like him stubborn and all
Fallon had an appointment with Doc Reeves one Wednesday morning
Her worst fear was coming to truth
She was pregnant with Mister Seager's baby
Scared and trembling she knew it was life changing
Wouldn't be able to hide her bump from anyone
She knew Botchie would flip and Geraldine would be upset too
Fallon wasn't sure how to tell Mister Seager
A Negro woman pregnant by a man that was every bit of lily white
Fallon told Bobby about the life they created together
Bobby wasn't so happy and went on and on about
How this life was no life for a half-breed child living in this world
Bobby's family wouldn't accept Fallon
Poor girl struggled with right and wrong
She still saw Mister Seager every chance she could

Catching the number three bus from one side of town to the other
Until he no longer wanted to look at her
He didn't kiss her like he use to and there were no more room rentals
Near the river and most times he didn't even show up to meet Fallon
She was beginning to regret the baby and still hadn't told Botchie and
    Geraldine
One morning Fallon crawled out of bed
Crept out the door in shame as she made her way to Miss Leotha
Miss Leotha did homemade abortions for girls in trouble
With a wire hanger or something
So Fallon paid the forty dollars
Climbed up on the wooden table and let Miss Leotha scrape her insides out
Fallon bled all over like a red river and before you knew it
Fallon laid there lifeless
Miss Leotha screamed
No more baby or Fallon
Botchie and Geraldine had no clue
That Fallon was dead
Pregnant with a baby
Mister Seager's baby
Bobby as Fallon would call him

Brixton

Smack dead
In Brixton
Playing music
For my babe
Feeling good
As good can be
Babe rubbed
My shoulders down
While I listened
To the rain
Falling hard against
The cobblestone streets
Well I fell deep in love
With your wicked
British accent
I listened softly
While you tried to
Sing a tune
One thing led
To another thing
You placed your hands
In mine and it started
A fling
We did the things that
Lovers do
Being with you
Is everything
And everything is the truth
It ain't nothing in the world

If it can't be everything
Feeling good when I'm laying here
Sunken right next to you
You are what I call living
Living right here with me in
Our own little whatever it is
Here in
Brixton

Cake

My kisses are
Every bit of calypso
To the point one would
Believe that they were in Tobago
I've been told that my love is
As savory as the foods the Geechee's
Cooked down in Savannah and I
Would love to prepare you a plate
But I know that I can't and not to
Mention there is a valley that
Stands in our way, nevertheless
It never stops my mind from taking
A trip down the many blocks of
Memory lane where our eyes met
And your kisses were ackee and mangoes
While intertwined like Chilean grapevines
However I do wonder if you ever think of
Those moments such as I but they're so far gone
And who we once were to one another is
Now a folktale that's been passed on
Yet my heart is still as soft as the Louisiana cotton
That my ancestors once picked on the river's plantations
My faith in seeing you one day is as strong
As the bass in Paul Robeson's rendition of
"Ol Man River" however I tend to let go
Of that thought just to avoid another collision with
The demise of you and I all over again but I do know
That the unspoken words between us are as sweet as cake

Catamaran

I don't know
Where I'm going
I'm just here
Floating on the
Ocean's blue
Maybe the waves
Will take me to Cuba
Maybe they will
Take me to Peru
I couldn't think of
Anything I would
Rather be doing than
Laying here floating
On the catamaran
With eyes to the
Blue skies while
The seagulls dance
To mother nature's tune
I'm having an affair
With solace and I've
Longed for this moment
Everyone should have
Them a catamaran

Catch Back

The music was bumping
Crowd wasn't spirits naïve at all
Just like that
Out of the blue it happened
With no hint of anything
As far as I could remember
Before you knew it
I was all in with no reservations
Pulling a crime on someone because
A crime had been pulled on me
It's not that I didn't care but I
Just didn't have one care in the world
At least for that moment but it
Was time for me to get a
Few steps ahead of the game
And see the world through the
Tiring eyes like all of the others
But I wasn't worried because
As long as the music was bumping
And the liquid spirits were pouring
I still had a chance to get away with it
To take all that I could
In a matter of seconds
And didn't pay the idea of doing right
No never mind at all
Because it had been done to me
So I had to give that feeling of injustice
Back to anyone in sight so target
Was spotted and I took the shot

And like that the soul fell to the floor
As I watched without remorse
Crazy thing is that I didn't win a thing
For being so quick to react but now
I have inherited a life of looking over
My shoulders and hoping that
The bumping music and the crowds
That are not spirit naïve doesn't
Catch up to me but if they do
Then it's simply called
Catch back

Catching Hell

But I didn't mean to be a horrible man
I thought I was doing something
To keep up with the times
Shucking and jivin on the block
With Chester and Leroy
While I made my ways on over
To Nona's house with her fine ass
And after that over to Persa's for
Some of that fine ass she would give me too
Shit them both were my bitches at the time
Making me feel good in many ways
Probably the way I put the old mule down on em
Or the way I moaned when their mouths
Fitted around in an oval shape if you know
What I'm talking about but I didn't mean to be
A bad man and though I watched my daddy
Treat my momma the same way and she would
Always keep letting him back in and I knew it was wrong
Momma cried a many of nights and my brothers
And I cried along with her as her heart was breaking
I couldn't let Nona or Persa go especially after they
Both were pregnant at the same time with my children
Nona gave me a girl named Maureen
Persa gave me a son named Arthur
And for the life of me they wouldn't leave me alone
Wouldn't let me be at all and I had to divide my time
Between both shotgun homes on the same block
Miss Francis across the street said I was a good for nothing
Low life ass nigger and she was right
I was no good and no good to be with

Every bit of my daddy
Persa caught me at the park with Nona one evening
As little Arthur walked behind her and all hell broke a loose
Persa and Nona began to call each other every name in the book
Getting ready to come to blows
Arthur was crying and on top of that they both ganged up on
My ass and beat me from here to kingdom come
I mean they bust my lips and my nose and Nona
Was scratching my eyes out with her nails
I guess Heaven up above gave them some sense
That the problem wasn't with them but the problem
Was with me the old good for nothing low life ass nigger
Now I have no place to go but to sleep on my brother
Melvin's couch every night and I know his wife Lucille
Hates my fucking guts and to top it off I can't see
My fucking kids because them two bitches got me by the balls
Just why right now I'm here catching hell

Cocaine and The Man

Such a shame
He's in pain
Not this again
Who to blame
Nights of cold sweats
Days with regrets
Painted smile on
Inside a turmoil boils
Can't explain
The hard rains
He's going insane
A fix he needs
Pockets gone
Eight ball is home
Appears to be strong
Spirit beyond worn
Love can't save
The life he's made
Time in rage
When can't score again
Fiend and mean
An addicts dream
Mental chains
The life of
Cocaine and the man
Only to happen
Over again
A battle between
Righteous and sin

Hours of a binge
Lifted to the high
Remnants of years
Before consumption began
He's feeling caged
The poor man
Use to be sane
It happened
It blazed
A life
His strife
Living while dead
The life of
Cocaine and the man

Colorism

Separated
Placed into a box
By my own kin
Painted to be anything
But human with red blood
Confined to being less than
Reduced to being
Disfigured
Aesthetically distorted
Not fit for a magazine cover
No smash hit they say
In passing while being called
Midnight
Black so and so
You so black you blue
Black spook
Caged because I failed
The paper bag test
Yet I'm confused
Because we shared
The same womb
Fall asleep on top of
The same struggles
Can't even take the
Colored entrance nor
Sit anywhere on the bus
Let alone the back
Because in my case
The skin is a sin

Nothing fair about it
Yet it's the box
My own kin
Has placed me in
Sometimes I struggle
To get out of it
And there are times
I sit and wonder
When will we overcome

Congo Square

So breezy
Of a Louisiana night
I walked the cobblestones
In a time where I was free
And running wild
It was there
Right over there I saw you
Standing under the tree
I love you Congo Square
You brought me to a dream
Sweetest dream I ever seen
And it's all for me
So many times I wondered
Where it'll happen
And imagined a time where
I would be but never did I imagined
As I enjoy the nights breeze
I'll fall for love
Love falls for me
I love you Congo Square
Sweeter than a sweetest dream
I feel like heaven with moonlight beams
Never knew
Where the rituals took place
I'll be under a spell
Moving about steadily
And there it was waiting for me
Could it be all a dream
I love you Congo Square

Deeper than the seas
Love comes to me
Oceans breeze
Brown leaves
Sweetest dream I ever seen
And it's all for me
Congo Square

Corporate America

I walk in every morning
Polished and full of gleam
Knowledgeable of why I'm here
With strength and welcoming
But I can't stand around and smile
And talk about fancy trips to
Napa
Yellowstone or
To Martha's Vineyard while standing at
The watercooler with the Anglo's
Or how my father and I play
Golf every Sunday at the country club
There is no country club where I'm from
Other than the corner stores or the jail houses
There was no father neither but
I'm here to fill that mandated quota
That's the only reason there is
Not many of me here but I know why
They expect me to silence myself
And be glad that I was one of the chosen ones
While they barely whisper a good morning
Hello or
Afternoon to me
Walking right on by like they can't see
All of this six foot five melanin
And to thank the fancy office
That sits in the corner means
Much of nothing when one has
To walk in here and be on stage

A modern day minstrel
Smiling when I hate to
Talking about life
When our lives are not the same is
Trying to compare oranges to apples
Simply wearing
Everything but the black paint on my face
No place for a person of color
But no such thing in me quitting because
Beyond the walls of this joint
Lies the same struggles waiting for me
I can't afford to run
Damn shame not many of us are in here though
But that'll be too much like
Doing right

Country Day

I'm no rocket scientist
Nor am I a person
Of upper echelon descent
Nevertheless I do know some things
Things that are as
Clear as a country day
The ancestors up above
Have never stirred me wrong
I can almost taste whatever it is
I know those flavors that are
Bitter and sweet like I know
The lines of my black skin
I've been around to know
What I know and what I know
Is what I know because I've
Always known what was what and
That's a whole lot of knowing
About things
About self
My senses ignite into a rush
For some odd reason at times
I can't turn the blind eye to them
More importantly I use the third one
I know what I know
Because I know what I know
By the God's
I know what I have to do
When knowing is
Clear as a country day

Dear Married Woman

Dear married woman
This morning
We must part ways
Back to a life
Opposite of each other
Back to not knowing
That we exist
Now today
We both
Must deal with
Karma

Death

I don't know if
I'll be relieved of
My pains
Or if the promise land
Is actually the promise land
And I am in no hurry to find
Out just to let the good Lawd
Know and aware that I enjoy
The land in which I walk now
And as old folk
Continue to rant about
Going on to glory
I sit back and wonder
Has anyone come back
With a message or a postcard
Telling of the sweet times
Of the other side and if it's
Really a reunion of all my
Kin that have perished along the way
Not that I want to know anytime soon
Just to let the good Lawd know
That I enjoy air in my lungs
Whether it's full of smog or not
So an undertaker has no room
In my life at this current time
So all the wailings of
Precious Lawd take my hand
And leading me on is not
An adventure I tend to

Embark on until the time is
Right and I don't foresee that in
My vison anytime soon
Not until I'm gray all over
And I could no longer
Live the life
Of an invalid
At the hand of a caring facility
I much rather be here
Right now and maybe forever

Don't Shoot Me

Don't shoot me
My arms are held up high
All I have is this one life
Only crime I committed
Was looking you in your eyes
I know its hunting season
For you but I'm not ready to die
Don't' shoot me
Isn't enough you've been killing us
Since the beginning of time
Isn't it enough that our kids
Understands your hatred before
Knowing their nursery rhymes
Don't shoot me
I was just born here
Wasn't my choice to drag and link
My ancestors from one continent to another
Wasn't my choice to have you rape our mothers
I'm not the one in denial about you being my brother
Don't shoot me
I've done nothing but breathe the same as you
I've done nothing but live in my people's truth
Yet I am not afforded the same opportunities as you
But you insist on keeping me in the blues
Don't shoot me
I'm already wounded
Soul has more holes in it than the soles of my shoes
Only thing I've done was nothing to you
Only thing I know is that you get away with your truth

Killing me everyday
Erasing my existence down to the root
Don't' shoot me
I have no more blood to give
You've killed our kids
Been a menace over the years
Daylight comes
We all fear the picking season
Because we know it's near
And we wonder
Who's next

Dope Man Blues

Me gotta go and get this dough
Me gotta go and smoke this dope
Me gotta pawn what I can find
Me gotta snort this good ole line
Me gotta do what I gotta do
Me gotta sing the dope man blues
Me gotta carry my own pipe
Me gotta drink gin all night
Me gotta sell a little leg
Me gotta find a place to stay
Me gotta do what I gotta do
Me gotta sing the dope man blues
Lawd I sing the dope man truth
Lawd I can't get passed the tunes
Lawd I don't think I'm gonna change
Lawd I'm such a crazy man
Lawd I got my dope fiend crew
Lawd I sing the dope man blues
Me gotta get some help right now
Me gotta walk a great long mile
Me gotta find me a new home
Me gotta leave them streets alone
Me gotta learn to tell the truth
Me gotta sing the dope man blues

Eatonville

Hot musty Sunday
Sweetwater and friend chicken
Living in Eatonville
Don't feel like much
Living ain't easy
However I get my thrills
Being able to sit down
With the likes of Zora Neale
And her mysterious folklore
About lovers
About life
About lessons
With my heavy Louisiana accent
Listening to hymnals
Smoking on tobacco
Starring at the sun thinking about
All my could-have-been's
And all that I am not
How did I get to Eatonville
Gallivanting is what I call it
Wherever night caught me
Getting it how I live it
With a whole lot of
Cussing
Crying
Carrying on
Living ain't easy though
Southern must is real
Listening to the tales

Of the common folk
Enriched with blues
Like Zora Neale
I've become just another
Nappy head
Living in
Eatonville

Eight O'clock Pacific Time

Eight o'clock pacific time
As I stand gazing out at the
Mountains in the distance
My cup of java keeps me company
I'm in another moment of knowing
Another dimension of myself
Yet releasing another set of shackles from my mind
Just so I can walk with much more ease
Than I I've ever done before
I awoke to the realization that I've
Let them all win time after time
Taking my existence and creating
Me into something I didn't want to be
Nevertheless I was green and I wore that
Shade for a few seasons but now that
I have surpassed those moments those
Memories are embedded in me like
A dinosaur's fossil buried in the
Middle of the earth and I don't know
If I should try to cover up the permanent
Tattoo's or be proud of them like a parent
Standing in joy as their child graduates from
Some institution of learning but if only time
Was retractable they would have never won
Over the titles to
My mind
My walk
My core
So present day I'm feeling relieved

Much proud of who stands in the mirror
I got all my shit back
They didn't win at all
They just took the exact same things
Someone took from them and most of them
Never got any of it back
And maybe I'll leave time alone
Truth be honest I can't get them days back
Not sure if that would be wise
However
Eight o'clock pacific time
My day is just getting started

Eleanora

Love you Eleanora
Every bit of a *Holiday*
Gardenia in motion
Standing on the stoop
Of a brownstone in Harlem
Lady on any Day
Belting out the Blues
Better than any other tune
And although the late night
Hours are every bit of intoxicating
From the getaway pushed into
Your life lines
I can only seem to
Think that I just
Love you Eleanora
Hum a melody for me
While I make love to
Them There Eyes
And there is not a thing
Strange about the fruits of your chords
And I'll admit your edge is quite raunchy
Not to mention your language is more
Spicier than Louisiana cayenne
However I can't help to be
In overdrive behind you
Standing in front of your stoop
Hoping to catch a glimpse of you
Or maybe I can spot you at Carnegie

Sometime around the chill of November
Wonder if you was still here
What would you belt out for me
Or for any other that just
Love you Eleanora

F%#k You

I've learned
That what I want
Really doesn't matter
In the eyes of many
But only
In the sights of I
So I have to keep
My eyes on the prize
Knowing my ass
Is always on the line
And everyday
I have to strive
To go and make
This difference
Whatever that change
May be and so what
If you don't
Get me and
If you don't
Fuck you

Familiar Stranger

Everything I have
Is not always up for share
I always have to keep a
Little part of me for me
Just not into symmetry
In most cases the notion
Of being equal to are just
Thoughts that sounds good
When the words hit the air
And just like the wind
That thought blows on by
So in a sense we're all laying
Next to
Sitting with or
Loving a person
We barely know
A familiar stranger
Simply because we all haven't shared
Every part of our being and truth is
We just don't have to

Faye Mildred

Faye Mildred
Apple of
Dootie Miles' eyes
Loved her like
No other man
By day they were
Honeymooners
In the eyes of the
Other sharecroppers
She was the envy of
The fields amongst
The other women
Dootie Miles
Loved her and when
Those night skies
Came to existence
And the corn hooch
Flooded Dootie Miles
Blood stream
He became something
Faye Mildred had never
Seen before
Enraged by his own pains
Of being just a sharecropper
He began to inflict them
Onto her physically
The beatings became
A ritual of the nights
Behind the walls of

The old wooden shack
And after he whipped her
Like he was fighting
A nigger on the streets
Dootie Miles tried to leave and
Faye Mildred held onto him
For dear life
As if he didn't try to take hers
Promising him that it was
Okay to love her the only
Ways he knew how to
As long as he didn't leave
Well
One night as the hooch
Flooded his veins
And as the skies crept into
The weary night
Dootie Miles
Loved Faye Mildred
To death

Fiend

It's just no cause for this
Too early in the morning
I sit here starving to
Hit my next cloud again
Here I am longing and frothing
Everything is cosmic
The colors of every hue
Gliding on roller skates
As I inhale and release into
The atmosphere I'm numb
Fear I don't feel or concern
Of my whereabouts
I've walked naked down blocks
Conversing with self
Hair matted all over
While spectators scream or shout
If it's a cure for wanting
What I'm wanting
I don't want it
I have to get my fix
It's a devious current
It's a chemical trick
That makes me forget
The long list of rifts
The once upon a times
When I had such a mind
To get out and find
Anything but a high
I was alive but instead

My cravings rise
It's just no cause for this
Too early in the morning
I sit here starving to
Hit my next cloud again
Here I'm longing and frothing

Fool of The Year

I've heard it all before
The sounds of violins
As you speak your truth
And nothing is wrong with
Telling the truth however
Yours is a bit redundant
My ears bleed each time
But conflicted with
The fact of knowing
Oppose to not knowing
This is where I begin to
Question my words and
Decision to invite you in
From the wilderness
I guess that's why they say
That some animals are
Better suited to live in
The wild instead of
Trying to house a beast
That's incapable of
Being stable
Somehow after knowing
All that I know
Having been around
The block a few times
Honestly
Joke is on me

Biggest
Fool
Of
The
Year

Four Fathers

It's those
Undertones in
The choices of words
That fills me with fury
That turns my heart into stone
Questioning my abilities because
History has given you the right to do so
Exhausting how I prove my being
Day after day only to wake up to
Do it all over again while you
Watch as I am drenched in sweat and shame
From tending to the fields and making
Sure that you have enough vittles while
I barely have enough to fill at least
One corner of my stomach but I'm
Supposed to be happy when you
Call my name or appreciative when
You deliberately place sanctions on my life
Just because you can do that and I tell
You the God honest truth that I've grown
Terribly tired of your out of touched asses
And its bout time you come down to reality
Because we won't take it any longer while
You put on an act of enslavement in front of your kind
Only to sexually demean us when no one is looking
Stealing our existences as you've done forever
Creating a pseudo life based on generational lies
Basking in blessings that are pseudo
Not realizing you're fortunate from the slave trade

Of the strange fruit that decorated the
The trees like a Christmas ornament which
Is why I can't seem to fathom why many
Of mine could even lie down next to you
Procreating and deleting who we are from the
Face of this earth and you got the nerve to tell
Me that slavery has been over for hundreds of years
That no one see's the color lines anymore
But I got news for you and that is only the name
Changes but the mentality stays the same
Slavery is alive and well
It never went away
You can thank your four fathers for that

Free Me

Free me
Your twisted mind
Has kept me bound
You being around
Has kept me down
What it was between us
Has vanished away like
The memory of a life
That has succumbed
To dementia
Free me
Deep down I have
Kept you bound
Holding on to
What never was and
Probably suffocating
The life from your lungs
Though I didn't mean to
But you were all I had
And that hasn't been
much of nothing
So I'll remove my
Lock and key only
If you do the same
Free me
I don't want to be yours
Any longer

Frenchman Street

Give me a reason
To sit here and listen
To the music's
To be here and be
Aroused by the smell
Of roux and andouille as it
Forces its way onto the street
I wait like a bus is coming
I anticipate my wait won't be long
The streets are packed though
Probably hard for any vehicles
To get through so at this point
I just don't know
Ready to leave but
I don't want to leave
Give me a reason
To stay and become one
To feel whole again
With moments of endless forever's
Talks of what will be and
Making plans to be home together
Facing life as it comes
Like a violent surge of waters
I'm ready to leave
Somehow I can't
The smell of pralines reminds
Me of us intertwined like
Molasses and vanilla extract

So I guess I'll be here
People watching
What seems like forever
Right here on
Frenchman Street

Funky Good Time

This morning life was amazing
Watching the waves
Crash onto shore
Was like good ole music
Music that was funky in beat
I felt the notion
To stand and do my two step
But I kept it cool
Didn't want to alarm
The onlookers to the point
Of having them call a padded wagon
But I needed to dance
Just as sure as the waves crashed
I was sure I needed the music
To give me all those
Moments of life I
Lost along the way
To tell me all those
Things I wanted to hear
That never seemed to come
I didn't need a dance partner
Though I welcomed
Anyone that wanted to
Break free as well as me
The waves
Was everything and more
The earth that stood behind me
Was dull in its appearances
And I had no intensions on going back

So if the heavens that housed
My ancestors was willing
To give me the sight of seeing
Waves crashing onto shore
Like good funky music
To my ears
Then that's just what
It was going to be moving on
A good funk session
While I did my two step
Dancing and grooving
Into something new
Leaving the old parts
Of me behind

Good, Bad, Ugly

You really want to know me
Well here it goes
I'm mean
I'm happy
Sometimes in between
I can be vulgar like my mother
Heartless like my father again and again
I have dreams to remember
Shores to crash onto
Thoughts of yesteryear
Often makes me misty blue
I'm easy to love
When I'm getting my way
When things are not as easy
I often vanish away
I can be gypsy
Never know where life
Will catch me
Sometimes I sit when I pee
To avoid getting the floors wet
Don't have good aim
I don't mean to be rude
I'm inflicted sometimes
With shit and circumstances
I get angry at plowing fields
I feel no pain when
Getting lashings
I'm a good man
At least I believe

I'm a tough motherfucker
Often times in make believe
I have my ancestor's African features
Often times I play with danger
I get by how I know how
I'll be here for awhile
Don't consider me endangered
You wanted me
Well here I go
The good
The bad
The ugly
That's me
Being ashamed
Makes me no never mind

Got Plenty/Don't Got

I've got plenty
I don't got plenty
Just good and bad
Happy to give all my nickels
Then I'm broken and sad
I've got plenty
I don't got plenty
Got a lot to give
But then giving a fuck
Can be so much harm
And I don't want to live
I've got plenty
I don't got plenty
Let me be a friend
When I turn my back to you
The daggers from your hands sink in
I've got plenty
I don't got plenty
Honestly I don't know
What I have
Or what I don't have
I just know that
I've got plenty
I don't got plenty

Grapes on a Table

Grapes on a table
Saltine crackers
Sweet water and
My many thoughts
Chain smoking
The essence of who
I partially am away
Each puff at a time
It's hot outside and
I'm in a moment where
I'm on the horizon of
Something enormous I hope
Like finally being introduced
To the man in the mirror
I have not known him for
Quite some time now
And there are parts of me
That's tired of being left out of the loop
Being a man has so many connotations
Behind just being a man
It's sort of like just existing because we're here
Tends to get boring at times
This is how I know that there
Has to be something bigger than life
Waiting for me to discover it
I'm not talking loud music's
Finger popping
Shucking nor jiving but something
That is more defined

Like the lines in my face
Louder than any song played
Without betraying who I am or
Who I was brought here to be
Something bigger
Much more interesting
Than a bunch of green
Grapes on a table
I don't know what it is
I do know it's coming

Great Pretender

A façade
Dressed up in all the fixings
Smelling of a French fragrance
With mannerisms that was probably
Taught in a refining school of some sort
Impressed that the difference between
Salad and dinner forks were noticed
Everything that anyone should want
Guest of honor at all of the fancy teas
Where exquisite literatures were discussed
As well as delicate artworks
However when the skies turn into night
And the moon glazes the midnight streams
And all the makeup has been removed
You're home drinking your cocoa
Out of a chipped cup passed down
To you from your grandmother
While thin layers of tin
Of the scatter site in which you
Lament in dreams turned into nightmares
Protects you from the winters chill
And the only language spoken
Are the words of a drunken sinner
Singing the words of a Muddy Water's tune
Just to think
They don't know who you are
And you keep the depths of you

Away from the elite in which
You keep up your face in front of
Only to be more sad than the
Night before
As the moon glazes the streams

Gris-Gris

My mind wanders
As I stand in front
Of the broken mirror
Layering my skin
With old hand-me-downs
I retrieved from my neighbors
Trash can in the late night hours
I spray toilette water on me
I found in front of an old store
Smells like the kind my grandfather use to wear
I was a work of art
At least I thought
As I stared at my reflection
But I have something to do
I'm going to need all the help
That I could get
Knowingly I come from a
Long line of slaves
I tend to keep up
With the modern traditions
So that means anything
Is conquerable and I shall not
Be detoured away from my
Plan of actions
But before I go
I send a prayer out to
St. Jude
And I call on Gawd as well
But as sure as I was born

On the cobble-stoned streets
Of old Nawlins herself
I don't ever leave
My old box-cart of a home
Without my potion
My magic
My power behind the power
Of Gawd in heaven
That gets me on by
And when I have something to do
It gives me a boost
To get all that I need
I never leave home
Without it
Never without
My
Gris-Gris

Howling Like a Wolf

The wind chill is deadened
Howling like a wolf
In in my mind I was always yours
In flesh you were someone else's
From afar I watch and wave my hands
Whenever we caught a glimpse of one another
And you acknowledging with a hint of smile
Like always the smile fades and I continue to
Watch you from afar
In love
In happiness
In a time where time
Has been everything to you
Realizing I don't fit your mold
Often not a resemblance of your desire
Though we have moments
They never go any further than talks
Maybe it's a mutual emotion
Yet I've stop wondering many moons ago
I watch you from afar
Still waving in peace
Waiting for your hint of a smile
The wind chill is deadened
Howling like a wolf
In in my mind I was always yours
In flesh you were someone else's

I Don't Mind

My mind is stronger
Than a religious faith
My heart is cold as
The Alaskan migrate
I'm a loner
In a world full of fake
It isn't a wrong
That no one is home
With my time I won't pay
But
I don't mind
If you don't really want me
I don't really want you too
I'm glad that we didn't go through
So
I'm looking finer in the mirror these days
Smile for no reason
Long as my black legs
The love I offered
Expired in May
Now you've been
Knocking for long
But no one is home
In my bed there is no place
But
I don't mind
If you don't really want me
I don't really want you too
I'm glad that we didn't go through

And
I'm free from believing in you
Probably make me blue
What I come with
Is too much for you
To handle is too much
For you
But
I don't mind
If you don't really want me
I don't really want you too
I'm glad that we didn't go through

I Exfoliated

I stand before the mirror today
And I peeled away the layer of clothes
That's embedded onto my body
Because something in my heart
My spirit was just not right at all
As I peeled away each piece of clothing
I saw my many faces, my many journeys
And I peeled away so much that
I found myself looking at my
Image and I was a little boy again
A little boy with the knowledge
That I have now and I never
Felt so free and so at ease
My tears were happy tears, a major relief
I took my knowledge and vowed never
To walk the same lines ever again
It gets hard trying to walk on rugged terrain
I burned those old clothes by a fire
That I conjured up down by the bayou
And with every flame I erased away
Everything that was or what I considered
An impurity to my soul and by the gods
I didn't mind at all, not one bit
So now I can go on and finally live
What I call life after life
Amen

I Feel Good

I feel like
A sunny moment
On a country day
On the front
Porch drinking sweet
Tea and eating ham
Sandwiches while
The fragrance of
Green grass danced
In the air and pulling
Into the drive way
Were aunts and uncles
Not to mention all
The cousins and
Play cousins ready
For times shared
Doing much of nothing
And at some point
We knew the green beans
That Grandma Earlene
Were snapping would
Eventually be accompanied
By friend chicken
By potato salad
By Rice
By giblet gravy
And a table full of
Everyone while the
Kids sat at another table

Away from grown folk conversation
It was all love
All a part of the plan
How we groomed one another
To instill whatever it was
That was going to give
Us a piece of life although
There were always a few that
Strayed off and deviated
These moments were
A slice of pecan pie
With a scoop of homemade
Vanilla bean ice cream
Nothing fancy about it
Elegance had nothing
To do with it but we
Were together and although
We were miles and miles
Away from being perfect
We were together
I feel better than ever
I feel good

I Groove

I just get on with the groove
Yet I don't understand me
But that's the best part about me
Awkwardly understood
A bit of a recluse in my own rights
A bit of a fast talker on the flip side
Being me is all I know how to be
It's my weapon to survival
Strong and unbothered by much
With the mindset to withstand
Hurricane forced winds
And I've weathered the storm many times
However it's a struggle in progress
I just make it look easy
Though sometimes on the back end
I'm fidgeting like an old tree branch
But the music's that plays in my mind
Keeps me in stride
Keeps me wanting more
Keeps me prepared for war
Strategically I move
Because I have to
The world never afforded me comfort
And honestly I don't want it
Much rather be grounded and well defined
In my existence that changes like the seasons
So what if I have war wounds
I like when they are on display

Tells a story to the strangers
That passes me on by
Nevertheless I just groove
Dancing to my own rhythms
Best I know how

I Hate Math

I fell out of love with love
Seems so much easier
Been a struggle to get back
But
Can't say that I'm homesick
Or
Has it ever been a home
However
Whatever it's been
It's been all too complicated
Like a math equation and
Never been too good with math
The adding
The subtracting
Of my feelings
Of my concerns
Multiplying them with
Unbalanced souls and
Dividing me up into
Pieces of uncertainty
Is way too complicated
And
I could never figure out
Just what the final number
Should have been
Only constant thing is that
Love has been so blah
Most of all
I just
Hate
Math

I'm In Music

I'm in music
Samba like Jobim
Blues like Muddy
Mi Gente like Lavoe
I still hear the music
No matter how deep
The turmoil goes
I move to the rhythm
Of the conga
To the wailing of grief
From the low-down blues
I bare a tune for everything
No emotion left unturned
On the record box
I'm in music
My only escape to being
Who I am and facing
Circumstances I find myself in
Be it bliss
Be it agony or
Unsymmetrical in thought
I will not stop listening
Because when lives began to fade
Off into time
The music never does
It always stays the same

I'm Just Not....

I'm just not in love
I reckon I'm not
Going through anything
Just what it is
It's almost like being
On stage singing the same old songs
Night after night while the crowds
Shout in enjoyment
Waving their hands to
The sky testifying but I've not gotten that feeling
Haven't found that sweet emotion
It's too routined
Every day is the same
Same old dreams
Same old plans
Same cooked meals
Even the rejections are identical
Cookie cutter and parts
Of me want to feel guilty
That I'm not in need
However I just can't
I'm just not in love
Probably all loved out
I've paid my dues
Spend most of my check
Going for broke
Long story short
I'm just not in love

In the Raw

I don't have
Much to offer
But some time
For you to see
Me past the outer sketches
Of my existence
I can offer you
My wisdom in times of fog
I can tell you
What has made me bitter
I can give you moments
Of mental pleasures
However I wonder
Will this suffice
Will this be a full plate of food
Because I have plenty and
To know me
You have to know me
Parts intertwined by insecurities
Along the banks of glee
But I can offer you much
That doesn't cost
Too much but a little
Understanding
Emotions and honesty
And honestly
Here I am in the raw
With no contraceptives
So the only barriers

Are the ones
We place in between
What we have going
And like anyone else
On the block
This shit gets a bit
Confusing but
Somehow we fight
To see life through
Whatever that
May be

Insane Asylum

I'm home again
From the looms of stress
Days that colors me so blue
I'm too drowned out
Hustling for my pay
Doesn't seem like
Much to hold onto
My mind is just a mess
My worth is at a test
Not the man I use to be
But I confess
I'm feeling really crazy
Like an insane asylum
Every day is empty
Much more emptier than before
Padded walls so naked
Like an insane asylum
I may need a vacation
From the horrors of this world
The mirror stares
At my broken face
An image that
Is painted of gloom
I need to wrap up
All the time I've spent
Living outside a broken womb
My vision is more or less
A trip to Lucifer's den
A haze as it always been

But I confess
I'm feeling really crazy
Like an insane asylum
Every day is empty
Much more emptier than before
Padded walls so naked
Like an insane asylum
I may need a vacation
From the horrors of this world
A joy to this world it's never been
A joy to this world it's never been
A joy to this world it's never been
Like an INSANE ASYLUM

Irritable Man Syndrome

I woke up cross
Angry about the sun shining
Agitated with the thought of
Uttering a simple good morning
To anyone that came my way
Feeling like a bomb
Waiting to detonate over Hiroshima
Not needing a reason to do so
Mind is in every direction
But the right way
The muscles in my legs ache
My neck is tilted
Because I obviously slept unaligned
The looms of the work day ahead
Is piercing at my brains
I just want to spend the day
Inhaling the perfume of Mary Jane
And sip on spirits
Clear would be my choice
But I know that I can't
I have to be productive
But smiling right now pains me
Hurts me all the way down
To my nut sack
And the only words that
Continue to come to mind
And falls off of my tongue are
Fuck
Shit

Bitch
While drifting off down memory lane
Keeping a tab of every soul
That has pissed me off since
I can long remember
I just don't want to be bothered
I am in no shape to face
The outside world pretending to
Be put together when I'm not
I'm aching and I'm stuck in a mood
That only time will fix
But until then
I ain't no good
No better than a
Low down
No count
Good for nothing
So and so

It Is Me

Hello
It is me
You know the one
That kissed you
While you were asleep
Now today
We are just strangers
I look away
As you look away
When we walk on by
With the sweetness
Of your fragrance
Dancing on my senses
Don't let it be misunderstood
I don't love you
Never have
But if tempted to
I'm sure that I could
I just love the moments
That are silenced
Brief but meaning in depth
We know what we have
Even if it's for a few hours
The same hotel
The same room
The same time
The same laughs
The same lust
The same goodbye

Hello
It is me
The one that puts out
All of your fires
The one that sometimes
Loves your pillow talk
The one that you
Make sexual vows to
Every time that we meet
On the boulevards
Of one another's
Erogenous zones
Do you remember

Last Night I Made Love to a Stranger

Last night
I made love to a stranger
Because I was here with
My love bank on empty
I was in my feelings and
I just didn't know why
So the closes person
I could grab a hold to
I embraced and held for
The moment because I needed
Someone to need me
And that could touch me in the most
Intimate parts of my mind
Last night
I made love to a stranger
We didn't know anything
About one another and
We didn't feel the need to become
Familiar with one another
There was a job that needed to be completed
And I was long overdue for a promotion
I just wanted to be
Touched
Tasted
Held
Appreciated
It felt good to release my emotions

It was dark and warm and the only light there was
Was the light that seeped through the venetians from the moon
That way this stranger couldn't see my tears that rolled down my Moorish
    skin
Those tears of mines told my entire life story
I continued to lay back and let this person have a feast with my body
Last night
I made love to a stranger
And I didn't even ask for a name
I just didn't care to

Lemon

Declared moratorium
On wasted love making
And decided to love
What loves me in return
Not wasting my time
On all the faces that I
Can't even remember their
Names to fill in a void
Temporarily just until
The next one comes along
Only to look in the mirror
Not recognizing the
Stranger I've become
Had to stop the madness
No different than a
Crack using fiend on
The hunt for my next fixing
Gave it all up willingly
Love I was making
Every bit of poison
Whomever I chose to
Relinquish it to at the moment
Became a recipient of my venom
Was given my fair share
Of poison my damn self
And I knew I had to stop
Get to where I knew
The love would be every

Bit of love and never
Disappointing
Forcing me
Into being as sour
As a
Lemon

Let Me Be

I can look down the streets
Gazing into tomorrow
Seeing first light
Birds against the blue skies
Grass green in innocence
Life moving about
I can almost reach it
To hold it in my perception
And expect what is yet to come
But somehow
Yesterday won't let me be
Like a constant imprisonment
Dammit
Yesterday won't let me be

Libya

It's never changed
Though
Everyone is surprised at its existence
The chains
Red blood served with oppression
Dehumanizing a man because of
His melanin
His strong features
Placing pain on their shoulders
Inflicting fear in their souls
The year is different
Times are identical to the day
When Plymouth Rock were painted
With tears
With urine
With uncertainty of a new world
That was unkind
Libya is
Powerless and emptied of the belongings
In their souls
Yet no one cares
Because the world is focused on
The latest dance craze or
Who scored touchdowns
On football Sunday's
Killing our people
Again and again for sport
Us fighting back
Seems unheard of

There are power in numbers
The strongest revolt is long overdue
Like the will of Toussaint Louverture
We must stand for something
Other than false happiness and hollowed love
Be strong my dear Libya
Redemption is on the way

Living Forever

Living forever
That's the plan
Like a tree by the river
I shall not be moved
My throne is the world
A position I share with everyone
Living bare
With only the necessities I need
Water
Love
Piece of mind
With a centered core
I enjoy the green grass
In tuned with the blue skies
Warmth with the falling rain
Whatever it may be
The blueprint is what it is
Living forever
Not a dream unfulfilled
Or some folktale sung by Odetta
Just all factual
Air in my lungs
Forever in my eyes

London

London
Dorchester hotel
Home for a few
Decided to walk
Sloane Avenue
You asked me my name
I told you Ramone
Name came to mind
Suddenly
It's who I felt like being
Invited me to
Portobello Market
Found a cafe
On stage
You sung jazz
Nancy Wilson
Told me about
Plans
Stars
Moons
Rivers crossed
Not sure
If I was in love
But I was here
In London
All that mattered
All that jazz sung
Had me thinking
To stay behind

Give up my
American papers
In that moment
I was now home
But for
How long
Just ain't
No telling
With me

Lotus

I've lost it
May be gone forever
I can't say that I'm disturbed
The road was beyond long
But I was not in need
Of any of those things
I left behind
All I took with me
Was my mind
Grateful to know
That it was still in tact
After moments of damage
Probably by my own merits
Those times are gone
Buried like a corpse
And my new tongue
Gave the eulogy
I've lost it
Only to give birth
To a new birth
And rising sun
Just like the
Lotus flower
Emerging from a pond
Blooming in the mornings
And still by the
Afternoons

Loved You to Death

I loved you to death
For seasons
For moons
For moments
Just because we were free
Young and risk takers
Because we were
One and nothing
Stood in the ways
Of our wonder
One evening I surprised
You by coming home early
With flowers in hand
Smelling of the cologne
We purchased some time ago
With the intent to give
You what I so desired
To give you every moment
Of life if I could but from
The bedroom were
Sounds of pleasure
Whimpers of lust
The smell of heat
In the dead air
And in the hall closet
In a shoebox that sat
All the way to the back
Held my caliber
Before I knew it

The sounds of
Pleasures
The smell of beaded sweat
Were remnants of the past
As red blood splatted the headboard
Canvased the walls
My God
What have I done
We were supposed to be forever
How can we now
He bleeds on top of you
You're dead still
Eyes open with no breaths taken
I'm so sorry to have
Loved you to death

Loving Through the Storm

You know how I like it
Slow like simmering molasses
One candle lit enough to see
Each other's silhouette
Slow music
Blues preferably
Thunderstorms
No talking necessary
Submitting to each other
Love me in this moment
Like tomorrow is gone
Right now I have no
Insecurities for you to tear down
Our kisses taste like whiskey
The aroma in the room is lust
Marijuana with
No covers on the bed
An old sheet over the window
Hung with two nails as it
Drapes in the middle
Though a storm has blown through
I can still hear police sirens
I don't care about much
Just love the taste of you
The feeling I get as
Two bodies are connected
Immersed in secular controversy
In our lowest moments
We are as grand as can be

Never mind the rent is due
The refrigerator is on empty
With every thrust of emotions
We are unconquered
We are unbothered by life outside
Of the walls of this tenement
Still the mood is relentless
As we lie in heat both
From racing hormones
From the southern night
Never mind after this moment is over
We're back to living in shame

Lucea

Woke up in Lucea
To the sounds of a Woman
Humming a tune
With the likes of Rita Marley
The aroma of jerk seasoning
Was dancing in the air
As the catamarans in the far distance
Appeared to be gliding over the Caribbean
I'm everything in this moment
Feel like life here could be forever
At the rate I'm going
I wouldn't mind it at all
Lucea loves me
Only thing left in America
Was the coldness of life
The kind of cold that
Sinks into your bones
That is excruciating as ever
Therefore
I'm staying here
Lucea
She loves me
I'm long overdue

Manhattan Streets

Sidewalks and street signs
Just living in a daze
Feeling as careless as I can be
Thoughts of loving all night long
Next to reefer and drinks
Was nothing but alright with me
So I flagged down a taxi
Took a ride into Manhattan
Told the driver bring me somewhere
Where I can hear a tune
A few boroughs later I was dancing in time
Holding a stranger hand in mine
Singing every tune with the radio
Having fun just ain't no crime
It's sort of better than living the blues
Right now I just want nothing but to be free
Having fun with a good tune
Even if it's with a stranger then I do
Then the music and a stranger
Is everything to me
Fresh out of a taxi
In a sinning mind
Dancing in the Manhattan streets

McClendonville

Shepard died in a car crash last week
His momma Ella Mae who use to be
Married to Mister Alfred but he
Ran off with a Passe Blanc from
Port Sulphur has one foot in her grave
And she taking it bad at least that's
The word on the corners of McClendonville
Church bell rung and told all us the news
Leroy didn't seem to care a bit in the least
Especially since Loraine ran off with Shepard and
The other day over at Pearl Anne's sweetshop
Johnny Boy beat the hell out of Duke in
A game of dice while Aileen lay in the gutter
Drunker than Cooter Brown from whiskey
And not to mention stinking of piss
The chirren slid down the levee on
Cardboard as the shipbuilders from Todd's Shipyard
Got off from the last shift of the day talking bout
All that who shot john madness while the smell
Of butter beans with pickle meat and rice from
Big Rosie's house made all us hungry round here
Percy and his crew under the tree trying to fix that
Old beat up Buick that his cousin just so happened
To find one day that's what the corners saying here in McClendonville
Too much of nothing goes on here
However it's all we know round these parts
Whether it be sitting in front of the bar room
On the corner of Odeon and Patterson on Fridays

All the way down to walking up the avenue
Waiting for the Nomtoc to role seeing who we could see and giving
High-five's and talking all the jives
Nothing special bout it at all
It's just McClendonville

Meadger Evers

Just like that it was done
I fell victim to all of you
Torn and disillusioned by it all
But as I stood on my front lawn
You shot me dead with your love
Your unbroken love and spirit
Shot me dead while on my front lawn
As if I was Meadger Evers
Then you left never looking back
My heart blood stained
My eyes purged salty waters
You gave life to my eulogy
Leaving me for dead
After making me believe
I was loved by you
Cherished by you
Truth is I was scorned by you
Shot me dead with your love
Your unwelcoming love
Shot me dead while on my front lawn
As if I was Meadger Evers himself
It wasn't even my fault
Betrayed me
Deadened me
Assaulted my emotions
Not concerned with my existence
Left me stewing like old cabbage
Shot me dead with your love
Your tainted love
Shot me dead while on my front lawn
Just like Meadger Evers

Mister Rufus Regrets

I can't
Make it to dinner
With you
The thought of
Being at the table
Looking into
Them their eyes
Is plain ole suicide
Only crime committed
Is that I see you
Know you all too well
Let you take me places
Though you compliment
My stature
I wonder who else
Gets those same
Words and
Before you can compliment
Me too much and
Finding ourselves
In a long night
You in my arms
And I doing something
That would bring
Levels of heat to us both
I'll just decline
The offer
I can't
Make it to dinner
Because if I do attend
Neither you or I

Will go back
To our normal
Lives as the same
And I'll be passing
The days with a
Few regrets

Modern Man

I'm okay
Nothing fancy
Self sufficient
For the most part
Guess Momma did
A hell of a job
Along with the elders
I'm sane without criminal
Identities like some of my
Fellow brothers of
The concrete jungles
It makes me no better
No lower at all
I live with many struggles
The plaques on my walls
Says that I'm educated
And I am life wise for the most part
Many storms I've conquered
More internally
Than anything
Yet I still awake with a smile
Thankful to the
Most high that
Air is passing through
My lungs without the
Assistance of machinery
That I have a passport
With many stamps
Where I've been able to

Visit avenues and boulevards
Far from narcissistic
A bit more confident in
My footsteps and where I belong
I still prefer to drink
My hot cocoa out of
A chipped mug sometimes
I rather eat at the
Hole in the walls
If I decide to get fancy
I know what an Italian
Suit feels like over my back
But I prefer sweats and t-shirt
I guess I'm still today's
Modern man

My Greatest Inspirations

You know all of my many scars
And my greatest imperfections
You also know that morning
Is not my favorite time of day
Somehow you never left me
But I wouldn't call it love
Although I've never met it
So I may be oblivious to what it is
But I'm sure it's not love
Much more of a consistency though
And that along is all I have and
Come to know so like a panhandler
I take all that I can get and I ration
Because every day is not fulfilling
And all of my scars
And all of my greatest imperfections
Are now my greatest inspirations

My Mind & Coltrane

I lay around
Most times in calm
Sun ray creeps
Pass the venetians
While Coltrane
Plays on the record player
My skin may be a little ashy
Somehow I am not concerned
Because my mind is full
Of words and music
That feeds me all that I need
And as the music plays
I wonder about forever
And what does forever consist of
Deeper than meaningless materials
This I too know
However as bold as I can be
I admit that I am a bit timid
To relinquish my thoughts of forever
Into the universe
May be a bit overwhelming at times
But I know these are the moments
That anyone hardly sees of me
I could be at my most vulnerable
Wishing and not wishing
Hoping and ignoring
And remembering
The night before where I made love
To a silhouette with an accent
While hints of the moon light

Illuminated both of us
And I do believe that Coltrane
Was on the record player again that night
However I am not much
For being alone with my thoughts
Not for getting ahead or bedside myself
But moments like this
My thoughts and I
I want to share
I don't want to share
But I do want to share
A bit puzzling I know
However moments like this
Where I am my most vulnerable
More in tuned with the music
I prefer to divide the pie
Maybe with the same silhouette
While playing Coltrane

My Mother Is

My mother is
Feminist like Ntozake
Rough like Pat Parker
Lady like Rosa
Pyramid like Egypt
Grapevine like Chile
Revolutionary like Panther
Salsa like Celia
Blues like Nina
Soul like Etta
Flowing like the Mississippi
Busy like a big city
Hilarious like Josephine
Funky like Aretha's Rock Steady
Robust like C.J. Walker
Old gospel like Mahalia
Jook joint like Shug
Poised like Coretta
Feisty like Dinah
At times bass like Paul Robeson
Simply because she had to be
Mysterious like Eartha
Supreme like Motown
Queen like Cleopatra
Rough like pavement
Sweet like limes
My mother is
She who she had to be

A sting like a honey bee
Hearty like collard greens
Sweeter than sweet tea
My mother is
Woman

Myths

In a time
Where tomorrow
Is just a myth
For some of us
Myths sometimes
Carry a negative
Connotation
Considering the
Times I do believe
That the next hours
Aren't for certain
So I suggest to get
All the living in
I can stand
Though living
Ain't easy
Being on top
Of the ground
Oppose of having
The ground on top
Of me would always
Be my first option
No matter
How strenuous
Breathing becomes
Or maybe even
Knowing the next
Few seconds
Are possibly

Myths however
Those are seconds
And moments
That I must
Take a chance
And keep living
Though living
For the possibilities
Of myths
Aren't easy

Nairobi

Nairobi was a tall brown-skinned brotha that stood six-feet-two from the Irish Bayou of sweet New Orleans. His shoulders were broad and he had hair that carried waves from the Crescent City all the way to Tangipahoa parish. The women adored him for his southern charm and the massive way he commanded attention when he entered any room. Nairobi was anything but formal; a man that could hardly read or write but he knew how to get by with his Louisiana charm. His creole accent. His masculine voice that was soft as a summer's crop of cotton that grew around the old plantations. His insides were as deep as a puddle though. Each night he found an abandoned shotgun home where he held house with ladies of the nights while hot white candles sat on the broken mantle and burned for hours on end. They fornicated. They danced to make-believe music as they pushed that liquid gold into their veins. And as the effect of the high took precedence over the dark night and hollow rooms of the house, Nairobi became someone else. It sounded as if he was talking into tongues and his body began to move in rhythm and suddenly the room turned into a giant field that stood along the levees of the Mississippi River and he begin to dance as if he was performing an old African ritual that inducted him into manhood amongst villagers. His woman friend that watched was overjoyed with laughter as the screams of heroin raced through her. Nairobi always amazed her. With him she never felt as if she was a low classed, piss smelling whore that paved the cobblestone streets with her love potions. He was in a trance and the field that he was standing on became surrounded by flames and he became a warrior fighting for the fruits of his life and the women that tagged along side of him. That high was so powerful. He appeared to slump to the ground but as soon as he was about to flop, Nairobi bounced right back up and began to dance and chant as if he was a god. A man of the heavens. A spirit that entered your home and cured lonely women of her sexual neglect. The old shotgun house became a center of worship and chants just like Congo Square. They both became free and unchained; bound to nothing as they groped each other and spit the most explicit languages as the liquid gold heated up their erogenous zones. Nairobi a brotha that didn't have to live like he lived was just another fallen victim of the night life of old New Orleans. A life that was anything but gumbo or shucked oysters. But a life that was more of just being free to be who he really came to life to be. No matter how rich his skin was and the dominance of his accent, he was just plain ole Nairobi that stood tall and that was admired by all those southern women that loved him with their eyes and sweet thoughts of him playing a tune with his tongue along the surface of their clitorises. He was Nairobi a man that had no depth and sense of what life was during the daylight. Just a vessel that came alive as the skies grew into night and just like clock-work he became a warrior that chanted and that moved his body into a great rhythm on the big field as his whore cheered him on.

N-digo Blues

I don't feel like loving today
No mood for regimented rules
Try to give part of my heart
In return I get the **N-digo** blues
Sometimes I wished I didn't love you
Sometimes it feels like the great flood
Maybe I wouldn't have loved you at all
If I knew I would have to pay
The ultimate cost
I tell you
Life in the streets is a deserted scene
Lawd hem'mercy
Hard up, hard to love
Much of a nightmare to the sweetest dream
Right now I don't feel like loving you today
Your rules are too much of a set of rules
Seeing your image is too much too bare
Giving me more of the
N-digo blues
I swear to you
Not much room for me in your home
Long as he's there; long as you care
Loving you is every bit of wrong
Times I've been through
Times I guess you knew
Dreamt of you needing me
Instead I've been
Holding onto the
N-digo blues

New Year

The New Year
Is in the distance
Birth of new horizons
Time renewing itself
Nevertheless I have
All of my belongings packed
Ready for the world as I
Was for the previous year
My bags are packed with
Emotional stability
Spiritual understandings
Clean energy
Bouts of laughter
And a few seeds so that
I can plant a harvest
That way I'll never starve
For the presence of anyone

Nina Simone Eyes

Lady
I see your eyes
You sing
Before you cry
I wonder
What's on your mind
Don't tell me a lie
Looking at me with
Nina Simone eyes
Sing me a song
Whatever song you choose
With you I won't lose
Don't you even try
To apologize for
Who you are
Fancy like a
Brand new car
But yet I see your
Love dies
Looking at me with
Nina Simone eyes
Your touch is so deep
Your insides are furious
However I'm curious
To know what makes
You sometimes glorious
What's on your mind
Please don't cover up a lie
Hold my hands

I'm just your man
Ask me what I feel
Inside while
Looking at me with
Nina Simone eyes
Your hair is fro
Lipstick of burgundy
Words articulate
Jewelry exquisite
Still a cloud
Still a ride
Looking at me with
Nina Simone eyes

Not Difficult Neither

I don't know much
About feeling love
From another's hands
Other than mines
I'm usually my own
Companion and
Truth be honest
It's not the life I
Dreamt of when I was
Sprouting up into the
Man that I was becoming
When I stared into the mirror
Though I am not an easy love
I am not a difficult one neither
Just tend to get lost in translation
When looking back over the years
That were most times too much
Not about nothing
Nevertheless
I am here waiting
Bare in my feelings
Waiting for your hands
To feel
To learn your way of love
Through imagination
I can almost understand
What you can give me
I smile in excitement
Just a hint

Almost afraid to let myself
See me do so but if you have me
I'll come
I'll let go all concern and
Wear my smile
On the linings of my heart
Just
Bright enough for
You to see
Though I am not an easy love
I am not a difficult one neither

Nothing Else for Me to Do (But Wait for Morning)

Many understandings of what we just did
Me next to you
We with tears
It was so beautiful
And fruitful as they say
My mind is going crazy
Heaven was in my ways
And I don't know
What else to do
But to lay here
And wait for morning
I'm just going to lay here
And think back to a few minutes ago
Smile just a little bit
But somehow I still don't know
What are we going to do
We crossed that line
Of friends into lovers lane
Your scents are all over me
And I can't even complain
It feels so good
I'm still so nervous
But there is nothing
Else for me to do
But to lay here
And wait for morning

Nude

Early this morning
I gave you me
Bare
No vail
And you didn't cringe
At the sight of my scars
From my many lashings
Across my back
God knows
I was hesitant
Not many knew this
Part of me
My head was bowed
Not in shame but
More in relief
There were tears but
I couldn't go another night
Not knowing
If you could touch me
In my entirety but
Something about you
Is not too encrypted
I'm satisfied with that
I'm vulnerable with that
I'm in love with that
Trust in my words
It has not been a
Crystal stair however
It's all that have
Now my hands are here

If you want to journey
With me and
If you decide otherwise
I'll stand aside
To let life happen
As it may
Nevertheless
Early this morning
I gave you me
Bare
In the
Nude
Unashamed

Old Man River

Old man river
Something you need to know
The tide that use
To keep me bound
Just can't keep a hold of me anymore
I can't take
Another promise at my window pane
Pseudo
Go on and vanish away
Before I find myself
Round here in trouble
I'll let it all go
Right now
Right away
Because I live a life
That loves me all the time
I live in a life
As of now it's peace of mind

Overtime

I'm not fair
Enough to have
European eyes
Or small features
Like a crackerjack prize
Baptized with a Negro mind
I'm nappy all over
According to color lines
Can't wash my brains
To be a walking lie
No matter what
I cry Black Man cries
Like a fatherless boy
That can tie a tie
Sometimes I struggle
Living on Black people time
No choice but to claim mines
Everyday living has become a fine
Each time I watch the tube I die
Sad that even my brothers
Are trying to be a supermodels size
Poisoning who we are has become the crime
Truth of matter
Most don't care to realize
More we live more we try to
Be everything other than what we are
Unconsciously asleep in overtime

Panhandler

Don't bother me
With hang-ups
Inherited burdens
From your people
Trying to mold me
Into what I'll never become
All so that you can
Show off a trophy
In a tarnished case
You've been having
Since the days when you
Thought you were about something
Perpetrating your existence
Like you on and popping
When in actuality
You're off and dead
At least to me that is
The way I see it
Is that you serve no purpose
Especially when your soul is empty
Especially when your smile is decayed
Almost had me caught up into believing
But I'll tell you this
You tried to impose all your powerless efforts
To make me over
To make me right
To make me nice
When in all actuality
I was everything

To me
Always have been
Truth be told
Everything that I am
Is everything that you have tried to be
Ain't hitting on shit
But like a panhandler
Begging for coins
Beneath an overpass
You keep coming up short

Patience and I

My existence
Is not promised to
Stand still in forever
You know
Waiting for what could be only
If I comply with what's being served
Is quite foreign to me
Fortunately
I am not built that way
I want what I want now
Patience and I have never
Had a understanding of one another
Honestly
I just don't care to be friends
I gets what I want
And I don't stand in lines
If you know me
Then you should know that

Placebo

I thought
But I didn't get
It all tasted the same
Took many dosages
Efficacy was never proven
I was blinded
So when I felt the touch
I thought I felt a rush
It all prove not to be much
Guess I was randomly picked
I can take that
I can withdraw from this trial
Possibly against the investigator's
Wishes but I never been a fan of
Faux
So I can't accept
A touch
Or a heart
That is totally
Placebo

Plantation

The great injustice
The river plantation
Grounds were beautiful
An oasis in Wallace Louisiana
At least that's what it was called
By the owners of the men and women
That owned the black bodies that were herded
Like cattle up and down the fields of the great grounds
Days were hot as Louisiana peppers
The nights were immersed in fears
Deadened dreams of freedom
Acts of shameless rapes
Dismembering the minds
And the killing of souls
That had no choice but to smile
When times were drear
The screams from lashings
Danced along the ears of the white men
That spectated like they were looking at
A ferris wheel going in circles at a carnival
The kitchen house was filled
With heavyset women that cooked the meals
The little children were taught to plow the fields
Milk the cows and how to mind their manners
Everyone tried to avoid being hung like
Christmas ornaments in the oversized magnolia trees
Though it was the inevitable
Life had to go on as such and on
Sundays the people that were worn

Were allowed to worship to the skies above
In hope of a miracle landing at their feet
And afterwards back to the cabins for vittles and whatnot
Wasn't no love from the big house
Treated like peasants
The white man soulless eyes
Took the existence of the first people
From the Mother of all continents to transition
Into what would become the guilt of American history
All the reparations in the world
Couldn't afford the menacing years
Of the great deaths of the great
Civilizations that were forcibly
Packaged into this country

Ready, Willing & Able

Been a long time
Since I've driven
Into the weekend
Without a care
At first it was a bit
Startling to know
That this ride
Was the beginning
Of something new
After liberating my
Soul of what was old
And beating me down
Or I beating
Something down
Nevertheless I was
Feeling a new kind of
Living and for me
It was just what the
The universal God
Ordered and I wondered
What the days ahead
Held for me
What was in the cards
Then I decided not to care
Not worry about
First light because
First light could
Hold its own and I
Stayed in the moments

Of what was happening
At that given second
Of air passing through
My lungs and I no longer
Was worried with
What may never come
To be and I
Just wanted to
Live and keep
Living whatever
That may be
Truth be honest
If it meant giving up
Some things
Some souls
Some music's
Then I was
Ready
Willing and
Able

Rebirth of Beast

Now I'm a wild beast on the inside
Walking back into what I use to be
A time when I hadn't
Had any concerns for much of nothing
It's wrong but
I've been molded this way
I've let them make me this way
Turning me into something unrecognizable
An animal has been created
Wild beast that would mull
Anything in its way
A savage
Blood thirsty
I'm on the hunt
I'm on the run
I can't turn back though
Just look what
You've done to me
What I've allowed

Reintroducing Myself

I have a hard time
Keeping the truth of
Light from you not because
I possess anything that's worth
Putting away but probably
Because I become nervous
When I feel the need to
Induce vulnerability
When you're around
Honest to goodness
I just like the way it feels
Since life reintroduced us
However I just don't know
Maybe all that we are
Maybe all that we can be
May not be enough
However
It's a chance
I'm willing
To take
It's a trip
I'm willing
To make
Although
Time is not forever
I'll spend a lifetime
Reintroducing myself

To you
Over
And
Over
Again

Roulette Wheel

You've given me much dedication
You've let it be known
I was your proclamation
Doing what we do
Has been every bit of elations
Never once did you
Ever lose patience
You
Gave me a dream
That proved to be real
Gave me a power
That gave me chills
Ignited a fire
The flames have grown
I just want to bring you home
To wake up next to me
Give each other life
You become my neck
I become your eyes
All these things
That you do for me
I'm your ocean
You're my sea
Looking at you
What we going to do
Reality ain't easy
Just the way it is
What we going to do
When we catch a chill

It may be a gamble
Like a roulette wheel
You
Gave me a song
Other than the blues
Gave me a ration
I used for fuel
When in doubt
You made me believe
That I am
All you need
The bees flew around
Waiting for the blooms
Nature took over
I made the room
In this home
For you and me
Now it's all reality
Looking at you
What we going to do
Reality ain't easy
Just the way it is
What we going to do
When we catch a chill
It may be a gamble
Like a roulette wheel

Routine Stop

I hold up my hands
Trying to understand
Yet you not hearing
What I'm saying
If I move it'll be a
Shooting range
Heart is beating
You're insane
Saying things we
Shouldn't have never
Said and that's when
It suddenly hit me
The middle of daylight
It was just another
Police raid and here
I am looking like the
Many faces that went
Down in the trenches
Before me by the blue flu
But I'm holding up my hands
The only thing to understand
Is that I was living with melanin
Only act of a vicious crime
That all of my kin that came
Before me committed
I can't understand
I can't begin to understand
Your uniform
Your badge

You're so derange
Protect and serve me
The richness and
Kinky of my hair
It's not sin
I'm just another black man
Life is in the hands of
Another uniformed man

Rummage Sale

The lights came on
And I'm feeling strong
A little anxious because
I know what I have to do today
I'm having a rummage sale
Getting rid of all these
Old boxes that surrounds
My inner being
No need to hold onto
Things that don't need to be kept
No need to hold onto the souls
That already decided to step
Everything must go
I call it my getting up
Getting out and getting over sale
I'm not even going to try
And rummage through this shit anymore
It was never mines to keep anyway
No sale is final
Today I can beat any price
There is a box of music, letters
Jars of tears, crates of pain and
Trunks of disappointment and
Let me tell you, if no one wants to buy it
Then I'm giving it for free
I don't want any of it anymore
It shouldn't have been mines to start with
Then maybe, just maybe
After I get rid of all these things

Then maybe I can learn
How to let go
Instead of harboring
What I don't need
Especially of people

Run Slave, Just Run

Gets cold
Down by the river banks
When the sun sets
It gets very cold
Down by the river banks
You hear me
When the sun sets
Its why I can't stop
I've got to flee on
Lawd it gets cold
Frigid like
Down by the river banks
When the sun has
Gone on home
I've got to flee
Move without detection
Gets cold
Down by the river banks
When the sun sets

Secular

Today I left the pulpit
And I headed on down to
The juke-joint that lined
The banks of the river
So that I could turn in
My taste of communion
For a flask of gin and give back
My Clara Ward spirituals for a Muddy Waters
Record and I didn't care who recognized me
Just for a moment I wanted to be of the world
And consume all of those things that I preach
To the public about that is hurting our souls
And making God ashamed of us but I didn't care
For the moment, I just get so tired of being a holy roller
And yes I prefer to be out here back-sliding like the rest
I left the pulpit today and right now I just don't give a damn
Tired of being perfect and honored as if I was God himself
Just let me be with all the rest of the sinners out here
I won't sneak and invite the towns whore into my bedroom
She will walk in my front door and so what if I live next to
Sister Blake, who heads the Deaconess Board and yes today
I left the pulpit and I'll be back, I'm doing my thing though
And don't think for one minute that I don't recognize these
Troubled faces out here; the whole congregation is out here
With their snake skin shoes, mini-skirts, cigarettes and razors
Just in case some shit goes down but I'll be back on Sunday morning
Screaming, crying and praying to God on how good he is, only to be
Out there doing the same shit as everyone else
Yea well I just live in this world
I didn't make it

Shockoe Bottom

You can catch me down
In Shockoe Bottom
Walking the old historic
Streets that Poe once walked
And more so the streets
That are lined with markers
From the slave trails
While wearing my jeans
That are belled
Sunshades that blocks out
Any ray of light
Beanie on my head
Greeting every soul
That passes me by as
Brotha or Sista even though
We are no relation according
To the modern way of thinking
And you might catch me with a
Freshly rolled joint in my mouth
Trying to sing falsetto just like
Smokey Robinson and The Miracles
And If I feel like driving
I just hop on into my Cadillac Coupe Deville
That's park down on Main and 20th
Where everyone has an afro with a pick in it
Even the white folks found a way to fro their
Stringy, European hair all the way up
I'm not mad at them at all
I reckon if I was them I would want to

Imitate black folk much as much as I could
I mean as much as we dance and cook neck bones
Collards and hot water bread
Shit man
Black is all the way good in my book
And if anybody ask me my name
I tell them my momma named me Percy
But all my friends calls me Ali because
I've been known to whip a few asses
Now today I'm much more of a lover
Met me a fine woman named Laverne
And she knows how to please me
Shockoe Bottom is where I be at
Everyone knows to look for me
And just where to find me
I might be posted up in front of the
Liquor store talking to Bobby nem
About whatever but nevertheless
I'm in Shockoe Bottom

Shut Up

I'm not sure I believe
What was said
Fancying me with
Words that have been
Said to many has never
Given me much of a
Mental erection but
I guess it's just what it is
Words and more words
Warm air to say the lease
But all I have are assumptions
Which may be quite immature
If I may add however
I make no apologies
I'm not green by far
I'm not vulnerable neither
I'm just reckless with my thoughts
Definitely with my words
I don't care hardly none
I only believe
When the deed is taking place
When I hear whimpers of heat
Coming from you as I climb deep
Afterwards we smoke a joe
Then walk yourself to the door
It's bout all we have
I can be a bit puzzling
Estranged
Just who I am

No excuses but I just
Don't believe in words that are
Too manicured
And deep down inside
That are not meant for me
So just
shut up

Spell on You

I put a spell on you
To make you want me
I light a candle for you
Like Marie taught me
Some people call it a root
It's just magic on the black market
I chant in Congo Square for you
Most times without you knowing
My potion breaks every rule
It's strong and it's working
I put a spell on you
And I want you to know it
A bag of spices for you
You bet not fight it
Mystery and scandal it's true
This juju is working
What's a conjure man to do
The drums are crooning
I put a spell on you
You got to want me

Street Walker Loses His High

I'm cross
And the music was too slow
For a moment of adventure
Suffocating my insides
To the point of despair
But I know I have to crawl
Out of this abyss of nothingness
To regain that brightness
That so many spectators count on
And I do have an image to uphold
So any look other than joy
Could chase my clientele away
And I've worked too hard
To get things the way I want them
To let it die like a big let down
The minute I catch my break
I'll have to revamp my set
Can't go on wearing the same color
This time I may dance
I may even sing
Whatever it is
Somethings got to give
Can't be so sunken
Like this for much longer
I'll call my connect
To get me up again
It's hard living in the
Sober
World

Strip Tease

You like when I move like that
To the music so freely
I give you fantasy and laughs
You get at home barely
You like the ways I perform
I give it to you
Before you're gone
While I grind for you
I give you chills
What am I to you
It can't be real
While I grind for you
It's just a hustle for me
I'll give you laughs
And spirits
And for a charge
A piece of me
Or we can keep it
As a strip tease
Put your hands on my back
I'll call out your name
Whisper sexual nothings
In your ears
Put you on your knees
I'm in control
But just ask
What I can do for you
You like my feel
As I strip for you

I give you chills
What you are to me
Is just a number please
Maybe I'll dance for
You a bit longer or more
Or we can just keep this
As a strip tease

Summer Cleaning

That pile
Of faces
And old
Use-to-be's
Just move it
All to the side
For the
Garbage men
No sense
In keeping all
That shit
With me

The Ancestors

The ancestors are talking
Warning us that
A storm is near
Everyone should take cover
The unknown brings about
Many fears
Some of us to endless tears
It appears that there has
Been a disturbance in the
Skies that hovers above
This is caused because
The land in which we walk
On is no longer fertile
And condemned by the hands
Of man ignoring the fact
That sweat, blood and tears
Are the reasons that there is
Earth beneath our feet
We're in the thick of thunder
The wind sounds like the
Mourning of a baby's death
The ancestors are speaking
Voices are raised
Authority is in full control
We've not made them proud
Our eyes are the color of guilt
Our pride is stained with shame
We've ignored the warnings
Completely oblivious to the teachings

Now we're headed to condemnation
Sadly knowing that we've done it
To ourselves
I only hope to the ancestors above
That forgiveness
Shall be bestowed
Upon us but somehow
I know that time has
Expired and the only life
To be expected is the life
Left over after the grounds
Have perished
Completely

The Great Depression

Which way to start
Because I'm almost through
And ain't nobody left around these parts
I tried to head up the road but I didn't get far
And the price of crude rises past harm
Man we only human
And all my paychecks added together just ain't going to conquer that
I ain't a slave man
No matter how much you don't like that
Which way to start because I'm almost through
It could be a cold winter night
Making a life on fertile land
Now-a-days, the man ain't the man
It's the man standing behind the man that has my land by its legs
Because I'm almost through
And ain't nobody left around these parts
Tried to head up the road
But I didn't get far
Cause the price of crude rose past harm

The Hook-Up

Today I'm in my own reality
My own little nasty world .....

I didn't know her name
I didn't care to have any emotional
Attachment towards her
And I bet any riches she felt the same about me
So we were speaking the same unspoken language
She straddled me
So she could feel the existence of my manhood
Lurk around her erogenous zones before entrance
Our kisses were warm and sweet like guava
I refuse to hold back, giving here nothing less than
An award winning performance
So she let me take her to paradise
With my tongue exploring every inch of her natural treasure
And the ways her back arched as I played Marco Polo
Pushed me to go even harder, turning my pelvis area
Into a diesel engine as I thrust harder and harder
I think she may have been West-Indian because words were
Heavy and I could barely understand but I knew it was patois
However I just didn't mind it all

Today I'm in my own reality
My own little nasty world .....

The Muses

I'm in love with the muses
Often finding myself
Living in a creativity
That only my mind can provide
Better than anything else
Most times a ride
Down the coast of what
Could possibly be and I
Don't need much company
Truth be honest I like it that way
Therefore I can be where I want to be
Without the misinformed illusions
Of a straggler whose purpose is solely
Created to tear away my many looks
It's no surprise that I am
Not a many of things on purpose
Tend to don't fit many molds
Reasons why I dream solo
In many colors and not being
Worried about my muses
Being taking away by a bandit
In the northern nights

The Plane Ride

The plane ride
Brings out another side
Memories so vividly
Like the time I told
Mama what happened to me
Plane ride
Teary eyes and inside
I'm still alive but not the same
I don't feel shamed
Who I am is just who I am
Bitter and sweet
Both instilled in me
I don't like goodbye's though
I was ready this time
My life is not my life
When I feel troubled
When I feel confined
The plane ride
Was just another time
When my eyes cried
Didn't have to wonder why
I knew deep down inside
Up here in the air I'm free
Down on sunken grounds
I'm more like leaves fallen
From a shaken tree
This is why I can say goodbye
Hitch me a plane ride
To another life

What happened to me
It just happened to me
But I cry on plane rides
My memories
Came so vividly
This time I let the rains
Fall endlessly
Summer rains
And there was no pain
The plane ride
Brings out another side

The Tour Is Over

I've been doing it
For far too long
Many nights
Singing those songs
To the same audience
To the same face
I've grown tired
I've gotten bored
With the St. Louis Blues
With the Louisiana Blues
With the Chicago Blues
With the you're all I need
I love you today
Don't touch me tomorrow
Laid up with me on Sunday
Creeping around on me on Monday
Deadened blues or
Any resemblance to the Blues
Not sure how this is going
To be taken
Honestly
I'm not concerned
Sure the crowd
Won't even notice
But as of tonight
The tour is over

The Window

My usual spot
Could be in a better place
Maybe, maybe not
I'm not amused by the many twist & turns that I've taken
But please believe me, it's never been by choice
But more by circumstance
My own people's blood laid out my path
To whatever, whenever and I don't like that
By no means
All I could do is wave at the life that was on the other side of the pane
The outside looking in
Maybe an eternity in this spot
Maybe not
I don't know how to groove on Sunday afternoons
No time to play on Saturday nights
I have to worry about tomorrow
Because nothing is there to take the worry
From me
For me
My usual spot
Could be in a better place
Maybe
Maybe not

Tired of Walking

You were always mine
The words we told each other
As we walked down Claiborne Avenue
Hand and hand facing the world
As we saw it passing before our eyes
Made me feel ten feet tall
When other men admired
Your coke bottle figure and the silkiness
Of your black mane
You were always mine
Since the first time I saw you
Sitting on the porch talking
With Genevieve Lawson
While her mother Miss Eartha Mae
Snapped beans and chew snuff
Gave me thoughts of forever
You smiled at me every chance you could
I embraced with coverings of security
Like any man would do for his woman
As we're walking Willie Rankin pulls alongside
In his Pacer that his father Mister Herman
Got him with money he won from playing the numbers
Whistling and shouting out what he considered sweet nothings and acting
     a fool
Nigga was blowing his horn making a scene
Look like to me the whole Claiborne Avenue stood still watching
I started to pull my blade out right then and there
Though I didn't have much and we both were on foot
I was still considered a terrible muthafucka at times and my woman
Was off limits to anyone so when I called his hands

Asking him what his problem was and if he wanted to hold court
Baby got all scared telling me to ignore Willie Rankin but I just couldn't
I wanted to fuck something up right here right now
Before I knew it she let my hand go and walked over to his car
I just knew she was about to slap the piss out of him
Cuss him out calling him everything but a child of God
Still gripping my blade that was in my left pocket
Ready to cut this nigga
Baby got in the car with Willie Rankin
And I'm confused watching her and as I started to approach the blue Pacer
Baby looked at me in shame with tears in eyes and told me
That she was tired of walking

To The Lions

You were not equipped
To have understood my real
Coming from where I come from
There is honor amongst thieves
Clearly you must have known
How critical transparency was
So when I opened the doors
To the kingdom and allowed
You to sit at the tables to break bread
Your only job was to give me loyalty
To respect the monarch
Simple as that
The laws of the land
But just like any peasant found in
The gutters I had to understand
Your mindset and that
Your only mission was to get ahead
Even if meant chopping my hands
The one that built bridges for you
Gave you a defined existence
Polished you but because
I'm so cleaver nevertheless one of the reasons
I was chosen as head of state
I kept my third eye open
Especially as you walked the corridors of the palace
When you thought no one was watching
However
I know everything
I've seen it all

So my duty to myself and to the people
Of the kingdom is to protect it
I shall do so at all costs
I shall not be angered
So the guards will escort you away
Before you leave you will be prepared
For one last feast in my honor so
To the lions you go
I'm sure they will find you to
Be quite scrumptious

Tonight (Mood)

I just don't want to.

Universal God

The Universal God
Is calling me to a much
Higher platform at the moment
The world as I once knew it
Prove to be the devil in disguise
I shall not bow down to
The European images I was
Brought up to believe were my
Saviors in order to dance behind
The gates of a promise that was
Stolen from my beaten ancestors
I don't plan on being beaten any longer
Or condemned by the eyes of
The old time teachings because
I tend to over eat at times
And indulge in lustrous moments
I am only human
The Universal God
Has made us all this way

Unwanted Stranger

What are you
Where did you come from
Thanks but no thanks
I didn't order any of this
But still you found
Your way next to me
And like my shadow
I have to carry you around
As if you are a baby and I'm your parent
I didn't put myself on this avenue to receive you
I always walked away
I always made a way
But yet and still
I'm here and now we
Are a couple, the dream-team
Someone has to send me back for revisions
This life I never envisioned
Walked around with many restrictions
I wish your birth was in remission
But that don't seem to be the case these days
And I don't believe in self-abortions
Why are you here
I never asked for you
Nor did I order your gifts
But I know you
Just can't leave

With the Devil

Tonight
I'm going to tango
With the devil
And I want to get
Out of control
I want to drive
In the fast lane
Make a few friends
Along the way
If I become an enemy
I'm just going to be that way
Let me live
Let me get high as the mountains
Let me go around to fountains
Drinking the brews of the serpent
I'll be a force to be reckon with
Dangerously I live
I want to be in the moment
To headline the performance
I am free
As a lion in the jungle
A few loves
I'm going to try to juggle
Walk the streets
That are pebbled
While I tango
The night away
With the devil

Wolves of The Concrete Jungle

Lonnie Boo and Grover
Sweethearts of the Ghetto
She had skin the color of amaretto
He had eyes that were bold and black
All the girls of the projects loved Grover
Not one of those jive turkeys could
Ever come close to getting Lonnie Boo
Inseparable they were
Her man
His woman
Would do anything for one another
One day Lonnie Boo told Grover
She wanted to see his bad side
Wanted to know if he could howl
At the moon like all the other wolves
Of the concrete jungle and every day
She pressured him to turn in his
Gentle side in exchange for war stripes
Grover began to cuss
Grover began to drink
Grover began to shuck and jive
He was what Lonnie Boo wanted
And she did for a few seconds
Until Peetey Dawson caught her eye
Around the corner on Murl street
He was more wolf than Grover
He already had his war wounds

So Lonnie Boo dropped Grover like
A habit she was trying to kick
But one Saturday Grover saw Lonnie Boo
On the avenue all fancied up and he
Managed to get her in his Pacer
Took her for a ride across the lake
Wooded area far from the ghetto
To a little shack where Lonnie Boo
Became confused as in what was about
To go down between her and Grover
So just like that he made her lay down
On the old beat up mattress and lit white
Candles and told her all those sweet things
He knew Peetey Dawson hadn't and she began to
Softened up and just as she got comfortable
He took his big hands and pressured them
Around her neck until she was no longer
A part of the world and Grover stood over
Her lifeless flesh and began to howl like
The other wolves of the concrete jungle